Gloss

Wisconsin Poetry Series

Edited by Ronald Wallace

Gloss

REBECCA HAZELTON

THE UNIVERSITY OF WISCONSIN PRESS

Publication of this book has been made possible, in part, through support from the Brittingham Trust.

The University of Wisconsin Press
1930 Monroe Street, 3rd Floor
Madison, Wisconsin 53711-2059
uwpress.wisc.edu

Gray's Inn House, 127 Clerkenwell Road
London EC1R 5DB, United Kingdom
eurospanbookstore.com

Printed in the United States of America

This book may be available in a digital edition.

Library of Congress Cataloging-in-Publication Data

Names: Hazelton, Rebecca, 1978- author.
Title: Gloss / Rebecca Hazelton.
Other titles: Wisconsin poetry series.
Description: Madison, Wisconsin : The University of Wisconsin Press, [2019] |
    Series: Wisconsin poetry series
Identifiers: LCCN 2018040962 | ISBN 9780299321642 (pbk. : alk. paper)
Subjects: | LCGFT: Poetry.
Classification: LCC PS3608.A9884 G56 2019 | DDC 811/.6—dc23
LC record available at https://lccn.loc.gov/2018040962

A portrait is a painting with a little something wrong about the mouth.

—*John Singer Sargent*

CONTENTS

PART III | SELF-PORTRAITS

ACKNOWLEDGMENTS

Many thanks to the following journals and magazines for publishing earlier versions of these poems.

32 Poems: "My Big Unsubtle Feelings"

Beloit Poetry Journal: "The Mind Revises. The Mind Takes Away."

Catch Up: "When He Is a Woman"

Compose Journal: "I Animal You"

Cossack Review: "To Make the New Loss Old"

Four Way Review: "Homewreckers"

Gulf Coast: "Group Sex"

Hopkins Review: "Group Text"

Horsethief: "The Contractual Obligation Movie," "The Room Where They Are Lawless," and "In the Room Where I Am Beautiful"

Kenyon Review Online: "The Room Where There Is Still Love"

Lemon Hound: "Cover"

Missouri Review: "We'll Fix It in Post"

New American Writing: "Bound Like Isaac"

The Pinch: "Recast"

Pleiades: "Largest Hands"

Ploughshares "Recast, Again"

Poetry: "Trying Fourleggedness"

Sixth Finch: "Do Not Want"

Southern Indiana Review: "Composition," "Gunpowder," and "Head with Open Mouth"

Tupelo Quarterly: "Love Poem"

Upstreet: "Soft Revolution"

Vinyl Poetry: "Make Good," "Self-Portrait as Thing in the Forest," and "In the Garden before They Were Animals"

This manuscript also contains poems that originally appeared in the chapbooks *Bad Star* (2013) and *Tender Trapper* (2012).

Thanks to Chloe Benjamin, Brittany Cavallaro, Oliver de la Paz, Rebecca Dunham, Matthew Guenette, Ashley Keyser, Alan Michael Parker, Emilia Phillips, Jimin Seo, KMA Sullivan, Emily Temple, Corey Van Landingham, Ross White, and Marcus Wicker for their feedback on this manuscript or poems within it.

And special thanks to Mark Stafford, my first and best reader.

PART I

ADAPTATIONS

GROUP SEX

There's you and your lover and there's also his idea
of who you are in this moment, and your idea of who
he should be, both of these like both of you but better—
poreless skin, flushed lips, hairless where convenient.
It's awkward, the theatrical way your lover throws back
his head, and should you as well? What if you're facedown?
The other him, the one who never forgets to roll the garbage can
to the curb the night before pickup, he would never let his right eye
droop upon climax, he would never smack your bottom afterwards
and say "good horse." He never has to give her the what for.
Her hair is always clean and she doesn't bring up the past
like a sopping lobster trap every time the two of them
are finally moving forward. She sees a wider vista.
You could watch the two of them all day—those toned limbs,
the faint perfume rising from their skin like ozone after a storm,
like roses bred to excess until the blooms break the canes—
you could watch her raise her hand to touch his face, softly,
as if she cannot believe he shaved for her,
as if there's only just the two of them in the world now.

HOMEWRECKERS

Say hi to California for me. Say hi to lovely weather.
I hear your movie is a good one. Your movie is a winner.

Say good morning to the good girl beside you. Say hello
to good decisions. The bread and the toast it becomes.

The sweet unction of jam and the dull knife that spreads.
There are ratings for content and there are ratings

for effectiveness. Give this breakfast a thumbs-up, give this
daily bread an *M* for Mature. You are no longer the man

who wakes in his own sick. You are a clean and gleaming
example of the benefits of benefits, the outcome of income.

Hello car. Hello driveway. My goodness it's been forever
since we gridlocked together, since we were caught in a pattern

and sidelined. Hello burning vehicle. Hello tire smoke.
Use your turn signal when passing. Politeness is a virtue

is a virtuous man. LA is a town and LA is a set piece
for noir and incest. I hear you bought all the orange groves.

I hear you're a pipeline and a girl with a fresh nose job.
You inhale and she inhales the good day the good life

what a good idea to inhale when the smog isn't smog
when it's potential good-bye good-bye.

RECAST

Every morning you are new to the world a bright flick of sun
on the pillowcase wiped clean of the previous day like a film cutting
to a fresh scene with a different actress and no one asking what happened
to the old one if she is waiting to resume her part or set on a shelf
in her dressing room I suppose no one needs to know a woman
after she's said her lines in the romantic rain or in the glaring lights
of a delivery room after she's moved the story along and the child
pushed out do you suppose she'd have something to say but the script doesn't
mention whether she steps out every morning new to the world
like a lick of some prior act of which you can't remember the taste
the script doesn't mention her exit or whether the music rises
like an ocean at night pulled along in the wake of a fat moon
and an inclination to keep moving it only says you've been cast
in the role of a woman waking up again and again to her life
with a look of total surprise to be there once more once more
entering the role you'd thought you'd left behind

GROUP TEXT

with lines from Kafka, Valery, Goethe, and Bertrand Russell

Can you believe is the question and Chloe says no
but Chloe is the ingénue and wakes up believing
so we laugh and she says no really and we laugh
again but what is belief in this context says Emily
and what is the color of our belief says Brittany
and if we believe then what do we get asks Corey
because if belief's not about what you get then what?
There's a pause before the words come, an ellipses
waving from the shore—Chloe says she could believe
if belief didn't really mean anything but it does
so she doesn't and we don't laugh and Emily says
belief isn't so much content as it is trust
that someone is listening so Brittany sends a pic
of her cat, Molly, and Corey says are you there, Becky,
but I'm just three dots, shimmering. I can't tell them
that my belief is a coat with the pockets shot through
but almost as if she could read my thoughts
laid out across the screen Brittany says that which
has been believed by everyone always and everywhere
has every chance of being false, plus here's a link
to an electric blue skater dress and Corey says
oh how sweet it is to hear one's own convictions
from another's lips (and texts a smiling poop
+ a rocket). Chloe says guys wtf a belief
is like a guillotine just as heavy just as light.

No says Brittany no one knows what a belief is
no one knows what a fact is and no one knows
what sort of agreement between them
would make a belief true. I've gotta motor
says Chloe the light just changed says Corey
losing service says Emily and Brittany says the dots
are swarming and I say to no one I believe I'm one
in a million droplets in a cloud of girls hanging over the city.

WHY I DON'T BELIEVE

I knit a baby out of spare cells and now
that baby isn't a baby anymore but a baby boy
but a boy walking. His male cells star my brain
and make him always a part of me. In the morning
he doesn't want me to pick him up but wants his father.
He shies away from my arms. I am in an unequal relationship
with a toddler. In the afternoon, my son lies down
on a large piece of paper and I try to trace him
with a crayon. I read on the internet
that children like you to draw spooky copies of them.
We never get much past the head before he laughs
and rolls away. I want him to be still so I can steal
a silhouette of his body right now this very second before
he's someone else. He gestures for me to trace my hand
and I do. He looks at the green crayon tracing, at my hand,
then his own. A copy, I say and he shakes his head. No.

COVER

Halfway through the mission, the operative called
his handler and told her the children
in the park he could see from the clerestory
were flying kites with tails decorated with ribbon
and foil. They are putting a real emphasis on aesthetics,
he told her. Some of us are born with priorities,
and the rest of us make due with aerodynamics.
Where's the package, she wanted to know.
He told her the smell after a rain is produced
by soil-dwelling bacteria, and there are oils on plants
after dry spells that rise into the air and hover.
I always thought, she said, that was ozone, and asphalt.
It's that too, he said. Your perfume is like rubber
on asphalt after a rain. Where is the package, she asked,
and don't say things like that. Someone is always
listening. There are these women pushing strollers.
They walk in unison. Where is the package,
she asked. Petrichor, he said. Petrichor is the name
of that smell after rain. There's this one kid, he said,
off by himself with a radio-controlled airplane.
That was me. The kid, she said, picturing him
as a serious child, maybe with glasses, though
he had perfect vision, and always had.
No, the plane, he said, I'm the plane.

LARGEST HANDS

In the dollhouse there is a momma and a poppa and a plate of glassy ham
and sometimes, when it can be found, there is a porcelain dog
whose mouth is open in a perpetual begging smile.
Where are the children? They were too expensive.
But the dinette set is lovely, the glass apples unpoisoned,
and as daughters are cheaper eventually there will be one.
At night, the sense that there are greater hands orchestrating
their every move, that there is a divine someone who cares
if their polished hair should chip, retreats, and darkness
steals through the small hallways, the bedrooms, and with it
come the smaller hands of mice, pawing through the master's
library, pulling down the tiny books and scattering
the leaves. One mouse snuffles outside the bedroom
and the momma and poppa shudder their unclosing
eyes, wishing that some force might move them
closer together, so that they might click their limbs
together for comfort. In the morning, the civilized
napkins, the table cloth, the fork and knife just so,
promise there will be breakfast and lunch and dinner forever,
and the momma and the poppa bow their heads to pray
a prayer of the finest bone china, a lacy white
that could only come from death's barest infusion.

COMPOSITION

The body is a mass of hair and teeth
        that walks and talks. Three hundred and five bones then two-o-six.
Two parts oxygen, one part fire. A child
        has all his life's teeth in his head, waiting to descend.
Impermanence is pushed out. Everything after
        is a commitment. Vast rooms of empty space between atoms.
Vast rooms in a suburban mansion
        which is a metaphor for late stage capitalism
and also the body. Blood is a connective tissue
        made of cells and cell fragments and liquid. A gallon
of milk is a body's blood. It's something
        to cry over. You are made from clay or carbon or one cell
ate another cell and the second cell
        didn't notice. This happened billions of cells ago.
So it was your mother's cells met your father's
        at a church picnic and no one noticed how the wind picked up
and scattered the paper plates.
        You might be forgiven for thinking there's an order to things.
This applies to childbirth and this applies to love.
        Two parts gin, one part Luxardo. The connective tissue
is a cord and our bodies are breath and fire
        yoked together. We are never easy with what ties us.
A mother's body is one part then two
        parts ever after; departure is the slowest part
in part because it's already over.

THE CONTRACTUAL OBLIGATION MOVIE

Every night the credits roll. The actors retire
to their separate trailers and call their agents.
Nothing was as promised. The flowers
in the vase aren't white but red and wilting
seems like the only response to the costume
designer's work. You must change your
wife, says the lawyer, and it's true, the terms
of the prenup are drawing near. But this one
seemed different, didn't she? In the mornings
she was already up, waiting for you with coffee.
Who will screen the scripts when she's gone?
If not for her, you'd have taken that dinosaur
movie. You would have waved your T-Rex arms.
It's hard to emote under prosthetics.
You're bigger than that, she'd told you.
Bigger than a T-Rex? you'd said. It's hard to imagine
her at forty, which is the problem. No one
who is anyone is forty. At least you aren't locked
in to being a dinosaur like some people.
You can be anything you want. That's the magic
of acting like a grown-up. You should send her
somewhere nice before the paperwork arrives,
show her just how big you can be.

THE MIND REVISES.
THE MIND TAKES AWAY.

When I think of you I erase most of what you say and replace
it with a courtly love poem in the style of one of the lesser knights
following King Arthur around; it's you, sans stutter or stammer,
precise like a piano's hammer—but gentle, gentle—
you'd be a soft pedal kind of guy. Last time we talked wasn't anything
I wanted to hear because I was tired, you were tired, and there were
no bulbs in the fixtures that hadn't at least contemplated going out.
I have contemplated going out into the silken night in my best
silken kimono and doing nightly things with silken bodies,
but I have not, mostly. When I think of the last ten years, I revise
us into a story of Saul to Paul—meeting you was one bright fall
off a horse and I woke up converted. I get to be a glowing cloud
of good intentions, not the sullen backslider you know.
And sometimes your hat is black and your spurs prick my ass.
Sometimes you are a white hat who sunsets away, and we never
consummate our unspoken hot for one another. Why, I cannot say.

HEAD WITH OPEN MOUTH

It's not real the story of the horses frozen solid
midway through the black pond their heads
cutting through the ice the ice cutting through
their necks it's not real the story of how they ran
from a fire through the woods all of them black
except for the white fog steaming from their nostrils
then into the pond the lake the ocean into the waves
where the water was so pure it snapped solid
at their impurity their desire their aching need
to escape it's one more way we are punished
for wanting the story to be real the story
where there's a path that leads to an open field
where the horses crash through the lake to the other shore

WE'LL FIX IT IN POST

Please ignore the leopard. The leopard is a continuity issue
we're aware of. We're aware the lead actor has one leg
in the first scene and two legs in the second. There are issues
with setting in the third. There is no possible way the light
across the kitchen table could be that golden, or the lead
actress could look so—the notes here say bereft?—when
learning of her husband's affair. The affair feels cheap.
Let's give him cancer instead. No. Keep the affair,
and give *her* cancer. We'll begin with a close-up on the shunt
in her chest. So brave. Her first tattoo a black pinprick
for radiation. Now let's have that golden light again—
can she be a blonde? Get makeup on this—then pan out
to the other sad sacks in the chemo chairs. Then farther.
Let's take a tour down the hospital halls. I want suffering
front and center, but clean. No bedpans. No vomit.
A few marijuana jokes here. Maybe a wacky doctor.
Then let's have the lead actor show up to say he's sorry;
he's so sorry that he's had a leg removed to show solidarity.
I think we can make this work. Let's cut in the leopard
stalking the halls but keep it clear of the children's wing.
The leopard isn't a metaphor for death. There's nothing
stalking us. This is a standard three-act structure.
The craft table is always replenished. Everyone here is union.

LOVE POEM

Sometimes you are the more elegant
of the two cigarettes in the cut-glass ashtray.
Sometimes you are the smoke curling up

in the slow frame rate, cutting to mist
on a dark road rising. I feel such elation
when you grab my wrist and demand to know

about the diamonds or the carved falcon
made of diamonds painted black or when my wrist
in your fist compresses to diamond from this mess

of carbon I walk in. I wear my hair over one eye
to avoid depth. I drive my sister's car.
She'll take the rap for any wrong turns

en route to the rented flat where you photograph
me in a dragon-armed chair against chinoiserie.
I was always an orchid coddled in the warmth.

It's not a problem that you cock your gun
at the small of my sister's back. She has a way of walking
that invites a man to try his aim. I don't mind

the shallow nature of our lines. They're still a pleasure
to mouth. You don't need ropes anymore, or any
restraint. You can leave your hat on the table.

RECAST, AGAIN

You are your father's broad back
                    rewrit in small script. Your feet, like his,
grasp the soil, confident
        the planet will never spin too fast
                and throw you off.

I never was so sure. I spent most of my childhood watching
                the clouds
                revolve while I stayed still.

                In this way, I was always an observer. In this way,
                        it didn't matter
        if I watched my mother crawl
                the hallway's length
                        on her hands and knees
        while my father yelled

                        or watched my father
                                put his face in his hands
                        at my mother's dramatics
                        while a phone rang unanswered.

        Both versions were true
        and neither could touch me.

I do not want anything to touch you.

I want you to know
the clouds move
because of the wind, not because
the ground is shifting.

It doesn't matter
whether she reached the phone
or if the phone's ringing was a detail
I added over the years.

For years, I told myself if I'd just answered the phone
a voice
on the other end would have told me
how to exit this scene,

but now I think I would have heard
your feet running toward me
through the wet grass.

PART II

COUNTERFEITS

TRYING FOURLEGGEDNESS

The boy and the girl were mostly gesture,
a clouded outline, the pencil lifting, lowering
to get at the idea of childhood, not the sour milk
and scraped knee of it. Her skirt was a swoop
of ink, his hand invisible in an undrawn pocket.
Circles make up the majority of the face. We are all circles
and planar suggestion. If the girl wants to be a horse
she need only walk into the outline of one
and line up her body with the chest. We'll fill in
the rest, and before you know it, she's a natural.
Who will ride her? The boy doesn't know how.
He has a hankering to sketch in a saddle.
When she tosses her head, he mocks up a bridle.
He mocks her. A bridle for a bride, he says,
which doesn't seem like what little boys say,
but he wasn't so little, and she didn't run away.

BEFORE SHE RINGS HIS DOOR

She is shameless,
     though shame will follow, and for a moment feels joy—
having walked a mile in deep snow
        past the aging townhomes,
past the community garden
        blasted by frost, the kiosk pinned with years
          of messages, apartments for let,
          bands to form, the lost
          and wanted,

past the frozen lake that could support a woman, a man,
        and the weight of their proximity,

past even the idea of herself as a woman walking
        to her own ruin,
an awareness she feels distantly
        inside her chest, raising its weak wings, hissing
like a crippled goose in the snow, his companions
          long gone,
keenly hearing
     the summer calling him home.

THE ROOM WHERE THEY ARE LAWLESS

With the formal negotiations done,
        with the papers signed
            and consent obtained,
    finally, the obligatory
      biting of the shoulder,
the standard toss
    of her across the bed
and the subsequent nuzzle
      which may result in but will not exceed
          two items of clothing tearing,

though in this as in all things
proper decorum must be maintained,
      for whomever has the floor
        retains it until yielding,
      and yielding is to be signaled
    by statements both verbal and non-,
as in speaking
the word "chrysanthemum"
      or tapping with the right hand
or the left
              (if specified
              in the initial negotiations)
    against
    one furred flank.

The act,

      which will henceforth in this document

be referred to as

love or

      mercy, will proceed

barring the following:

(1) suffocation,

(2) one or more limbs falling asleep,

(3) indifference,

(4) death, real or feigned,

and will continue as such until

both parties

consider themselves satisfied.

      (The terms of said satisfaction

          are set out in the attached appendixes,

       and may be revisited and renegotiated

     should either one

     or both parties

       desire.)

WHEN HE IS A WOMAN

When he is a woman I set his hair,
               the brown strands
               exit the comb's teeth
               gold, spill down his shoulders
       to a slender waist I put my hands around
          when I want him to feel small.

               When he is a woman I am a man
and as a man I am aware
       of how to make his breath catch as I touch
             one freckled breast,
     as I unbuckle
         my buckle with a definitive air.

When he is a woman the love feels more
               real, his eyelashes more real, his mouth
        like an unkissed girl's more real,
                and I hold to the fiction
        he's never known another's hand
     sliding up his thigh, not this way,
or another mouth
     speaking these words that glide up his thoughts
the way a man declares
     a land claimed, and then there's a flag.

When he is a woman
       I feel optimistic,
             when he is in a dress that suits
     his small frame, when the heels
          he walks in put his round hips to sway,

all these things make the smoke hover
above my scotch
on the rocks.
In this, as in all things,
I am traditional.

MY BIG UNSUBTLE FEELINGS

When you wake in the bathtub
          surrounded by ice
your first thought
          will be that you are a crushed mint leaf
               in the world's largest julep

and I want to say I'm sorry
          I took your appendix
because I feared it would burst
               I fished out your spleen
to balance your humors
                    I stapled your stomach
               because I can't bear to imagine
                         you middle aged
                         and paunchy
and I spooled your intestines
               round a crank
to whittle your middle
               the better to put my hands around.

Haha very funny
          you might say now help me
                    get out
but I worried your calves
                    had ideas of leaving
so they are under the bed
          and your arms
               now hold me
               and never complain
or steal the covers

every morning
I pet your hair
on my pillow
I pet your tongue
I cover your eyes every night.

THE ROOM WHERE THERE
IS STILL LOVE

Because he was inside the outside
    garden seemed darker, the dark lawn
lit by the occasional firefly in a series of stills:
        One golden lawn chair, empty.
        One bird bath, empty.
None of it compelling, though once
he could see a late-night dinner
    at that rough-hewn table under the oak
    and a beer in a young woman's hand,
        the condensation running down her wrist
        and evaporating in the hot night,
but why that wrist, not another's,
    why that drop of moisture or his mouth's desire?
It was all the same as what he circled,
      in the center of the room
      the bed and the woman's
      hair across the pillow just as he'd left it,
      her hip's curve exaggerated
by her sleeping posture,
as when he awoke, still inside her, and there seemed no way
to wake her, and in that sleep she smiled
    as if something pleased her
and he couldn't remember if they'd ever spoken.
In the morning,
the room was a lattice of light,
the mockingbirds called and he sang right back
but they knew his song already, had a copy ready,
and carried it off as their own.

ANIMALS AT PLAY

After the bacchanal beginning,
                  when you sling me
               across the bed,

    after the ecstasy
    that formally requires me
        to bite your shoulder,

let's have you wear a beaked Venetian mask,
                so you can't kiss me
                  in public.

Let's have you try on my old prom dress,
      and let me curl and set your hair.

I was thinking you might balance
      on your hands, atop this brightly colored ball,
          wear this fez,
             and this sparkling vest.

Let's crack a whip for the audience's benefit,
      so you can have a moment
         of sudden clarity
           that things have gone too far.

Let's pretend to be with other people
    until we're with other people.

MAKE GOOD

Promise me there is an end

to this ever. Promise me the tulips that return

with black centers and lurid pollen

will waste and wither in the heat.

Promise me this Tom Collins glass

will sweat itself out. Promise me another.

Promise me another kiss

to my forehead, a sweating good-bye,

promise me you won't

come back. Promise me the rabbits

will starve in their burrows.

Promise me the rain coming down.

Promise me the fox kits will drown.

Promise me a house a car a gate

a small dog to wag when I come home.

Promise me a mailbox with my name on it.

Promise me a new name that suits me.

Promise me the dog won't die.

Promise me a mouse in the pantry and small droppings

in the food.

Promise me moths in the clothes,

the small holes that grow larger.

Promise me your hands tied

behind your back.

Promise me we'll laugh and laugh.

Promise me a child will shake out like pollen from a tulip.

                                 Promise me you aren't the man you promised.

Promise me that the hands I cut off and buried

                in the backyard were my hands.

Promise me they won't grow back.

IN THE ROOM WHERE I AM BEAUTIFUL

In this room we are equals
                to the moment pushed too far.
      In this room no one sleeps, no one dreams
of another room
          where bodies have recourse
              to outside intervention—

In this room, the words you speak
      scroll across the walls
          the story of *everything ends,*

though for a time, with your name pressed to my thigh
                like a curling iron,
      and your hand around my wrist,
    I'd forget the dripping faucet, the cat yowling outside the door,
or how after you'd let go I'd bruise
          for more of you,
how I'd echo after—

      everything? everything?—

         In this room the questions intersected
the definites
    and infected us both
    with doubt.
In this room, the plaster walls absorbed our breaths,
      the door locked to the key of *only you,*
and the clean-swept oak floor was a river
I drowned in every night
         when you held me under
    the body that held me after.

BOUND LIKE ISAAC

Bound like a sheep, horizontal
               pupil fixed
               to the earth,
I have been unknowing and pliant,
       worse, I have walked meekly behind
the hand carrying the ax,
       worse, I loved that hand,
       even as it sharpened
       the blade, I pressed
               my muzzle
           to its unyielding,
               lipped at bitter grain
           and called myself fortunate.
Bound like a calf
           trussed by the legs,
bound like a child
       to a tree and left calling
for my friends—

they were not my friends—

I stepped to
       when whistled at, I put my arms
           behind my back, I told myself
there was a greater love
       that might step in,
and then later, when no voice sounded,
              I was the real alone, alone.

IN THE GARDEN BEFORE THEY
WERE ANIMALS

He holds his thumb to the pulse
      in her neck, presses.
            I could make you lose consciousness, he said. *I could do that.*

                  She is not averse,
                      has no allegiance
                to the ornamental pears
                that burst into selected beauty
                all around them, releasing the scent
                of rotting meat—
The image of them in this garden,
      sprawled on the last grasses of summer
need not remain
          uncultivated.

There are grafts that have taken.
There are careful prunings.
                She interprets this last gesture
                  as kindness, not a threat.
      I could, she thinks he is saying, but I won't.

When she shifts her position and her hair falls around
      his face—
            again, the beauty
                takes precedence
            over any utility—
      he doesn't care
                if she shades his face
from the sun, just that she is, for a time, there.

I ANIMAL YOU

In the formerly our future, I saw a note
you passed to a passing animal. That animal
was not the quiet sort who could keep a secret.
The note said I was an animal and you were sick
of my musk. The note accused me of eating
the rosebush, of bounding over streams
and fouling them in the crossing, and that the dead
hound nailed to your kitchen door was not the act
of cruel boys but one of my crude attempts
at communication. What you write is true—
the cows won't give milk, and the cat comes home
with one ear. I am what you took me for
when you banished me to the backyard,
where I read your note by the moon, which is not
your face but tears the mad out of me all the same.

SOFT REVOLUTION

Morning comes to paradise just as here on earth—
       so it is that I imagine him walking
down a street much like the one I walk down now,

his same shoulders, his same gait that hurt me
            with my own tenderness
for its bewildered
movements.
           If there is still anger in the next world,

he will carry it with him as long as his arms are able,
        and as they will be perfect, it will be forever.

If there is still love then it is this horizon spilling
        over in a gold rush down his body, opening
           him like a long-clenched fist.

Give him such simmering heat
and light—
        while here on earth the sun retreats from this street,
these maples, and my skin registers the night.

THE ROOM WHERE HE REMEMBERS

He sometimes wakes and finds her hair
                    between his teeth.
      and feels again the horror
           of indecision—
        whether to pull the hair from his mouth and burn it,
                or add to the mass in his stomach.

        It has been a long time since he first tasted
          this and then under
             different circumstances.

Then, she had shaken her hair from its pins.
She'd let it fall over him and trace his skin.

In his hands it ran
          through his fingers. There was myrrh and something
       older; the hiss of it against his fingerprints
              was the moment before
        the needle in the record groove
    conjures a symphony.
No one listened. No one called it beautiful.

HOW DAMAGED

When waking to the wreckage is as easy as stretching
        out across the bed and feeling the warmth
    leaving the cooling depression—

    that knowledge
that no one is coming back, and no one wants to—

Sex is a motion that slips ships from docks
        when Helen is just one more woman
     shaped like an excuse.
Walls fall, but then, walls do
and afterward, the sky only looks broader,

    the horses on the horizon
    crammed with possibility.

TO MAKE THE NEW LOSS OLD

When we talk about how we die, swamped
by overgrowth in one way or another, our voices thin and wheedle,
    and the wind blowing over the cuts on our throats
    pipes out
    the received wisdom
of our parents, theirs—

        we promise each other
           some constant
    after this, an after to this ever—

There was a man I loved and when I was done
    I still remembered the hot surprise
of his face near mine,
        flushed with desire and disgust, demanding
    explanations for my inconstant
           weather.

For him, I became another
        disappointment. For me, the same.
But I remember
how he'd clear his throat
    before closing arguments,
        the long silence in the dark bedroom,
his grasping hands,

how there are days

when what climbs us also provides

a support,

when the choking leaves and the wisteria blossoms

like bunches of grapes

are a beautiful canopy,

a respite from the sun, from the voices singing *after, after*.

DOMINION

Maybe the light from the window is yours.
                    Certainly the bed
                  is a possession.
      Certainly these sheets
            are districted and bordered,
                  the imprint of a body—
          maybe it is your body—
                  within the bounds of your sway
measured and cordoned,
            accordingly,
and the birds and the fish—
          these are yours—
            and that which crawls,
                and that which pulls itself from the waters
and gasps on the shore,
          new to the sky's gray curve—
yours also—
          and the trees when they betray the wind
and the wind when it betrays the leaves,
            and so much
gives another away
        in this world and that's yours
                as well,
    your name is yours
        and all you can see—
           you own it, so own it.

DO NOT WANT

What the sky had to say in the dark thirty tune
        that the birds took up and *V*'d further,
or what the church bells pealed
         and repealed as commandment
to gather or pray or resign.
        The prints on my skin
        that were yours, were mine,
the bruises you left
on my arm,
       the satisfaction in harm for the asking
        or the gendarme you presented
when a man
with a lance was needed.

What the radio stuttered
what the front seat leaned
what the hand
in the crux of it faltered.
        Or the sense of myself
as a woman in a dress or the sense of myself
        unaltered or the sense of myself.
What the porch light saw
       what the neighbors knew
what the dog howled out
     to the street.
What a man felt in his fist when another man
     fell to his knees
      and the please of that sickening thump.

When my doorbell rang when all the doorbells rang
    the man who was ringing
only wanted the woman to answer.
When I answered the door I was not the woman
      he wanted the woman he wanted
        was hiding.
What he had to say to the dog that was barking
what she had to say to the uniformed men
what I had to say when you arrived and you held me
because I was fearful of the man
    of her fear of the fear that I'd be her
if you were a different man
      which eventually you were.

GUNPOWDER

What if I did request that incendiary
                    touch, the slow burn
        of too much, the bleaching kiss of a man
who twisted my mouth
        into the words he wanted to hear?
                        If it's written, it's written,
            but what's read differs.
What looks alchemical
                shakes out chemical, hundreds of years later,
rigor is revealed as metaphor,
            a story about
        a mixture of grains, ground in alcohol,
dried and packed—how I wanted
                to be more than process,
to be the bright impurity wronging the ratio.
                            Did I love him for his acrid smell?
        For the way he threatened to ignite
just by shuffling in, all three parts of him uneasy?
                        In friction, we see what rubs
            and what breaks off, and in the fiction
    we tell others, there is an explanation
                        for fire and its hungers.
        I said *love*, and that is a match.
            I said *believe me*, and that was powder.

PART III

SELF-PORTRAITS

SELF-PORTRAIT AS UNSENT LINES, UNSENT LETTER

Hello. Hello dear. Dear one. Dearest. Dear to whom
my concern draws near. I write to you from Oklahoma.
From a small town in Georgia, sweltering. Blue sky above,
clear. Gray day, train trestles. Night with no distinction
between the water and the sky except for stars and stars
reflected. I write to you with the ticking keyboard
of my smartphone. A pen in my hand. A pencil stub.
Paper folded and refolded. Dear one, I stutter to start.
This tongue can't shape the words. A mouth full of spit.
When I last spoke. When I last saw you. When I last spoke
to you I saw you for the first time in the shape
of the last time. Such a relief when a city block erupted
between us, then a stretch of street, then miles, blissful.
Still I write to you. I text. There is no emoticon denoting
the distance between a face and its expression.
I am enclosing a photograph. I am attaching an image.
I no longer love the way you block the light. I am not attached
to your feet. Every night while you slept I picked the stitches
free, but then I had to learn to walk again. I took this picture
of the empty bed so you'd remember the shape of my body,
so I could imagine my return.

SELF-PORTRAIT AS SNOW WHITE AND THE PUBLIC DOMAIN IP

At fourteen, you practice rolling your hips
and it's drag; at nineteen, you've got it down cold.
Now you're any mother who can look in the mirror
and see herself older than the day before,
can see the young girls walking by without seeing her,
their tank tops loose over one shoulder, their jean shorts
artfully frayed. Where will we go, the young women say,
and everywhere is the answer. A curated series of stills
tagged and cataloged. What I ate. What I wore.
Here is the beach in Kodachrome filter; here is the sun
snapped flat. What's left to learn at forty? A reflection
doesn't answer. Fairness is a child's notion of the world's motion.
It hardly matters what half of the apple you eat.

SELF-PORTRAIT AS THE GOOD WIFE

Every partner begins as an associate.

A partner holds the beloved's hair back at 3 a.m. when the beloved is fighting a case of norovirus, but an associate's presence from season to season is uncertain.

An associate moves from office to office.

A partner's office has a plaque on the door that can't be removed without calling maintenance.

Partners know a bond is greater when there is flight risk.

Partners know hard work is always rewarded.

You were an associate and then you made partner.

Are you sure you are not withholding evidence?

Consent is difficult to determine in the state of Illinois, but witnesses report you were fully vested.

Wouldn't the counselor agree your lingerie suggests you understand something of the eroticism of withholding?

The counselor isn't covered under a partner's health insurance.

Sometimes you leave halfway through a session and your partner throws up his hands.

Partners know hard work is always rewarded except when it isn't.

You have been scripting things, watching a woman in your clothes go through everyday motions.

The elevator doors open and shut and in between you silently sob.

This is melodrama, and the music in your head swells accordingly.

But you are not withholding evidence, currently.

If no one is witness to your tears, no one can attest to your character.

You are not under investigation, currently.

When you are called to speak, you will speak to the facts.

A partner cannot be compelled.

What he said or she said isn't relevant anymore.

Conjecture is for those with imagination.

SELF-PORTRAIT AS A VERY GOOD DAY

Behind dark glasses I am enormously present
                           wading in a pool of flickering light
              algal at the edges
                                like a sick green dream of California

where dragonflies dip and skim
           the surface of the lightly poisoned water
                            some of them
                   coupling on the fly
             as if sex weren't already awkward

when I fuck I hardly levitate at all
                  and when I dive
                beneath the water
        I want to be detached

               from the searing world above but how
                    does one stop caring

when there are so many
             voices calling
                  where are you where are you
           come up there are snacks

so I swim back
            to frozen grapes and lemonade
        to the teenaged boys strolling by
            with fishing poles and bait

while the young girls spin
        on tire swings and scream to go faster
as if there were some shortage in the world
                of speed or disaster

SELF-PORTRAIT AS POSTSCRIPT

And another thing
   another thing
  another thing spills out when I am a rosebush
   when I am a cascade of lyre bird plumage
this pumped-out plush the plus
   of the bloom the minus of the bud
  a still life studying
    the many pretty ways to die

if these swirling vines look like my hand pulling back
    please realize the black beyond I stand before
  is set to devour these words
     and your name
   is just one more syllable to swallow and lick
   this song my sign-off to the greater good

go down to where the downed and feathered
    flesh parts to a knife's
     introduction
find symmetry in the cock's comb
  in the glands starring the aureole

and if the moles on my body match the constellations
if the sky is the same in your world
as in mine, then it is as it was
    when the giant squids
unfurled in the dark depths
    and we've only a soft seaweed light
  squinted into a tube

such is the filigree of me
against the velvet
      my shy knees crossed against you
           and the once again and the never more.

SELF-PORTRAIT AS SCOUT LEADER

In the menagerie
strapped to my back,
> there are two of everything.
If you need a fox, I have that,
> if you need a lion to eat that fox,
> I have that, too.
> I have on my person
guides for survival
> in the harshest of climates.
> I can build a fire
> from a dried carrot
> and a turtle shell,
and with a flick from my trusty pocket knife,
> the edge of North America
> peels up like a plush carpet.
I keep mementos
> of you on my person. I wear your gloves
> to better understand your hands.
The necessities don't weigh me down. I am prepared.

This voice that once called to you
> packs up light as twine.

SELF-PORTRAIT AS EVERYTHING THAT RISES

macaroon sparrow, rococo finch—
        the painted birds don't fear
                flame, they waft
          on the pillowy heat
       peck the curling canvas
         with their sugar beaks
     and cock their heads
       outside the gold
       coffered ceiling
        at futurity

       while the real birds—
        the hawk and his
      ominous wingspan
         the vulture's
        ugly dignity
the officious hummingbird with his darning needle head
      —circle and weave
    and in their arrangement
        draw the eye upward
        to the center

as if to suggest
     a greater composition
       to the clouds' progress
across a sky dotted with billboards

as if to suggest
    birds are birds regardless

SELF-PORTRAIT AS A PAIR OF REPAIRED GLOVES

Broken, I'm less thought of
      than the fashionable
and untouched,

      and worn,
I'm less worn, and more
      passed over.

So when the hands I seek
      to emulate
withdraw, I empty and collapse—

      and when I'm worn out
from rough use,
      I submit to a stitch

along my backside
      so long as it draws me
tighter to a firm hand.

SELF-PORTRAIT THROUGH
A KEYHOLE

Excess leaves no room for feeling regret.
>Too much too much and my arm through a window.
Too much too much and my head shoots above trees.
>I grow so that other creatures might lose themselves
under my handkerchief or fill their lungs to brim with brine
>and my bad intent. I grow to monster better
and more thoroughly. I make no more apologies.
>I suffer no summons.
Every bird curses me homeward. This piglet at my breast
>grows more and more like a child each day.
No cake baked by man from woman born
>will small me now.

SELF-PORTRAIT WITH UNSEWN SHADOW

See me as a boy in the window, never pleasing,
     see me as the housebreaker, picklock, sick
with longing to steal
       you from your bedroom.

When my eyes cry that's salt—
       but I don't. When you cry
it's blackmail. It's girlhood. It's a plan.

See me as a thimble
     deep in your pocket. See me as what's left
      when the stitch is cut loose.

How did you brother the others? How did you button
         the fierce right out?
When you shut the window
it's the worst sort of adventure.
    O Darling, love as I knew it
      straddled me savagely,
   was a wife, a wife, a wife.

SELF-PORTRAIT WITH YOUR HEAD BETWEEN MY LEGS

Glazed in sweat, I'm in the hot tropics
    of Florida,
        where the geckos Velcro across
    the bedroom window
on fine invisible hairs,

        where a perfunctory promise
    hangs over us like a broken chandelier
too heavy
    to dismantle.

I watch the ceiling
        for cracks, a water stain
and try to imagine the happy
        kingdom,
    as if I could punch my own ticket
        just by wishing harder

but the princess sleeps and sleeps.

Say peach, say plum, say typical
        to split the velvet nap
        with a clumsy thumb:

so much depends on
        the idea of breakfast in bed
        versus the sloppy practice.

SELF-PORTRAIT AS TENDER MERCENARY

1   The places lovers meet encode in the body: the lake and the bench beside, the car and the pacing road, the zoo where the lone bear won't come out from the cave.

2   In a sure way that spoke to practice, he pulled her arm back and she in a rehearsed way let her eyes roll back. They both listened to her exhale.

3   The cord around a lover's wrist tells us to remember.

4   In the foreground, one man puts his hands around another man's throat. In the background, one man puts his hands around another man's throat.

5   One tiger falls onto another tiger. One elephant tramples another.

6   The cord around a lover's neck and the hand that leads the leash. A wadded piece of silk, damp from the tongue.

7   The second man is very still. He deserves what he deserves.

8   The script calls for a brutal fight. The actors are trained in feigning violence. She is trained to observe and pulse accordingly.

9   He holds his thumb to the pulse in her neck, presses. *I could make you lose consciousness*, he said. *I could do that.*

10   The deer sniffs the fallen doe. Get up.

11   If she unties the knot then who remembers? If she ties it to another set of
animals and walks them down another set of roads. If the bench is empty and
the lake empties of fish.

12   High up in the tree, he can't see her body, just the fruit she tosses down.

13   A wadded piece of silk, damp from the tongue.

14   The knife in her hand for the fruit. One animal to another.

15   The surest way to untie, the fastest.

SELF-PORTRAIT AS THING
IN THE FOREST

Behind this dress,
>   two women
>   in the mess of one body
>   hardly covered
>   by the stiff beauty
>   of lustrous rustle.

Behind these freckled breasts,
>   two hearts that rush the blood,
two divergent desires—

>   each twin to the unseemly split between predator
>   and prey,
the white pet-store rat
>   bred for the boa
>   and the boa that would remake
the Florida landscape in his ever expanding image—

If a container can't lull
>   its contents into some sense of contentment,
the glass breaks, and out rush the teeth.

>   If one woman is the call
to the other's answer
>   the answer is to keep calling and calling
into the swamp and humid,

to tie this sash of silk shot, plain weave,
           and secure
against a hunger
             that grows without natural enemy.
A desire uncurbed
       is a flagrant thing, is a woman
          in the mirror, seeing clearly.

NOTES

"Largest Hands" was inspired by Beatrix Potter's "A Tale of Two Bad Mice."

"We'll Fix it in Post" is for Paul Seetachitt and Barrington Smith-Seetachitt.

"Love Poem" is inspired by the Sternwood sisters in *The Big Sleep*, directed by Howard Hawks, though other film-noir references and tropes appear.

"Trying Fourleggedness" was inspired by the drawing/painting *Bookoo Tries Four-Leggedness* by Noah Saterstrom.

"To Make the New Loss Old" is an imitation of sorts of Robert Haas's "Meditation at Lagunitas."

The titles of "Self-Portrait as Snow White and the Public Domain IP" and "The Contractual Obligation Movie" are taken from an io9.com article by Charlie Jane Anders titled "*The Huntsman: Winter's War* Is So Bad It's Fantastically Wonderful."

"Self-Portrait as Postscript," "Self-Portrait as Scout Leader," "Self-Portrait as Everything That Rises," "Self-Portrait as Tender Mercenary," and "Self-Portrait as Thing in the Forest" were originally inspired by paintings of Julie Heffernan's that share the same titles. They are, very loosely, ekphrastic.

Wisconsin Poetry Series
Edited by Ronald Wallace

(B) = Winner of the Brittingham Prize in Poetry

(FP) = Winner of the Felix Pollak Prize in Poetry

(4L) = Winner of the Four Lakes Prize in Poetry

The Golden Coin (4L) • Alan Feldman

Immortality (4L) • Alan Feldman

A Sail to Great Island (FP) • Alan Feldman

The Word We Used for It (B) • Max Garland

A Field Guide to the Heavens (B) • Frank X. Gaspar

The Royal Baker's Daughter (FP) • Barbara Goldberg

Gloss • Rebecca Hazelton

Funny (FP) • Jennifer Michael Hecht

The Legend of Light (FP) • Bob Hicok

Sweet Ruin (B) • Tony Hoagland

Partially Excited States (FP) • Charles Hood

Ripe (FP) • Roy Jacobstein

Saving the Young Men of Vienna (B) • David Kirby

Falling Brick Kills Local Man (FP) • Mark Kraushaar

Last Seen (FP) • Jacqueline Jones LaMon

The Lightning That Strikes the Neighbors' House (FP) • Nick Lantz

You, Beast (B) • Nick Lantz

The Explosive Expert's Wife • Shara Lessley

The Unbeliever (B) • Lisa Lewis

Slow Joy (B) • Stephanie Marlis

Acts of Contortion (B) • Anna George Meek

Bardo (B) • Suzanne Paola

Meditations on Rising and Falling (B) • Philip Pardi

Old and New Testaments (B) • Lynn Powell

Season of the Second Thought (FP) • Lynn Powell

A Path between Houses (B) • Greg Rappleye

The Book of Hulga (FP) • Rita Mae Reese

Why Can't It Be Tenderness (FP) • Michelle Brittan Rosado

Don't Explain (FP) • Betsy Sholl

House of Sparrows: New and Selected Poems (4L) • Betsy Sholl

Late Psalm • Betsy Sholl

Otherwise Unseeable (4L) • Betsy Sholl

Blood Work (FP) • Matthew Siegel

The Year We Studied Women (FP) • Bruce Snider

Bird Skin Coat (B) • Angela Sorby

The Sleeve Waves (FP) • Angela Sorby

Wait (B) • Alison Stine

Hive (B) • Christina Stoddard

The Red Virgin: A Poem of Simone Weil (B) • Stephanie Strickland

The Room Where I Was Born (B) • Brian Teare

Fragments in Us: Recent and Earlier Poems (FP) • Dennis Trudell

The Apollonia Poems (4L) • Judith Vollmer

Level Green (B) • Judith Vollmer

Reactor • Judith Vollmer

Voodoo Inverso (FP) • Mark Wagenaar

Hot Popsicles • Charles Harper Webb

Liver (FP) • Charles Harper Webb

The Blue Hour (B) • Jennifer Whitaker

Centaur (B) • Greg Wrenn

Pocket Sundial (B) • Lisa Zeidner